Augusta de Grasse Stevens

The Lost Dauphin; Louis XVII

Or Onwarenhiiaki the Indian Iroquois Chief

Augusta de Grasse Stevens

The Lost Dauphin; Louis XVII
Or Onwarenhiiaki the Indian Iroquois Chief

ISBN/EAN: 9783337061234

Printed in Europe, USA, Canada, Australia, Japan

Cover: Foto ©ninafisch / pixelio.de

More available books at **www.hansebooks.com**

THE LOST DAUPHIN;

LOUIS XVII.

OR

ONWARENHIIAKI,

The Indian Iroquois Chief.

BY

A. DE GRASSE STEVENS,

Author of " Old Boston," " Weighed in the Balance," etc., etc.

GEORGE ALLEN,
SUNNYSIDE, ORPINGTON, KENT.
1887.
[*All rights reserved.*]

LIST OF PLATES.

LOUIS XVII.
 From the picture in the Bryan Gallery, New York . To face page 16

ELEAZAR WILLIAMS.
 Facsimile of Pencil Sketch, by Fagnani, from Original Portrait, by J. Stewart of Hartford in 1806. . . . To face page 64

THE REV. ELEAZAR WILLIAMS.
 From a Portrait by the Chevalier Fagnani . . To face page 104

THE LOST DAUPHIN.

"THERE is no historical truth against which obstinacy cannot raise many objections. Many people think themselves justified in asserting against an alleged historical fact its improbability, without considering that nothing is true or untrue in the eye of history because it is probable or improbable, but simply because, assuming its general logical possibility, it can be proved to be or not to be a fact."

On first reading these words there would seem to be but little or no connection between them and the American Exhibition now open to the

English public. And yet no more intangible and inconsequent are the threads that bind together historical sequences and issues, than is this utterance of Von Bunsen's, which may well serve as a link between epoch and epoch, monarchical dynasty and Republican systems, the last scion of Royalty and an humble God-fearing missionary.

Perhaps of all the exhibits prepared by the American management at Earl's Court, none awakens keener interest or truer curiosity than the "Ranch" of "Buffalo Bill,"—his Indian chiefs and squaws,—their daily avocations, warfare, sports, and councils. The "red-skins" have always exercised a peculiar fascination over their English brothers. More than two hundred years have gone by since Governor Weymouth's two New England savages stalked about the streets of London, or that Pochahontas and her companions were made the idols of the hour, and feasted and toasted by every "Mohawk" of the day; while over a century has passed since Colonel Schuyler sailed from New York with his five Indian chiefs, selected, from the new Confederacy of the Five Nations, as hostages for the faith-keeping of their respective tribes. Used only as political agents in the hands of Colonel Schuyler, they were received at Court,—as was their Virginian princess before them,—where they made a speech duly prepared for them, in which they expressed devoted loyalty to the Queen, and hatred to the French.

Addison, in *The Spectator* of Friday, April 27th, 1711, writes of them as follows :—" When the four Indian kings were in this country, about a twelvemonth ago, I often mixed with the rabble and followed them a whole day together, being wonderfully struck with the sight of everything that is new and remarkable." He then pretends to have found at their lodgings, after their departure, a packet of papers, and proceeds to give some extracts from the "abundance of my odd observations which I find this little fraternity of kings made during their stay in the isle of Great Britain."

It was these Indian chiefs who formed the element of attraction at the grand review of outgoing troops held by King George III. at Clapham. The immense crowd gathered together on the Common came not so much to see the regiments—so soon setting forth to take part against the great rebellion of the American Colonies—as to gaze their fill upon the four native chiefs, who were the representatives of the aborigines of that Western land.

Their appearance was singular in the extreme, as they wore their native blankets and "wampums" over English clothes, with ensigns' breastplates, carried hatchets in their hands, and were in full war paint and feathers.

It may not be out of place to add that it was at this review that the new order was put in force, obliging all the troops, officers and men, during the American campaign, to dress alike, and their hair to be similarly arranged, in order that the rebels might not distinguish commissioned officers from privates; and the feature of the day was the presentation to all the regiments on review of felt caps with black feathers, in place of the old and more warlike head-gear.

It is not difficult to understand the interest thus awakened in Addison's mind, for no race of people—aborigines of any country—hold more of mystery, romance, and tragedy in their history than does that of the North American Indian. His character is a study well worth time and patience; in it are mingled, with almost impartial distribution, the attributes of chivalry, fidelity, treachery, generosity, pusillanimity, courage, fear, ferocity, and gentleness. Pages of the deepest and most thrilling interest could be written concerning this fast vanishing race, who combine with savage existence a knowledge of some of the arts and sciences of modern civilization. Testimony of their skill in model-building has lately been found in the opening of some aboriginal graves on Pilley's Island, Notre Dame Bay, Newfoundland. In one was discovered the well-preserved skull of an adult, which exhibited all the "peculiar characteristerics of the skull of a savage, but so well shaped and developed, it was difficult to suppose these Bethuks (or Red Indians) were of a low type of humanity, taking the intelligent contour of the head as evidence." Among other very beautiful articles of stone and bone work wrapped in birch-bark, found in the graves, was a perfect model of a bark canoe, as finished in every detail as if it had been the work of a nineteenth century artizan.

These, then, are the people who once owned the British possessions of Newfoundland, and who roamed at will, lords of creation, from the rock-bound coast of New England to the soft-rolling rivers of the Carolinas, and who spread their several tribes across the whole broad American Continent from the Atlantic to the Pacific.

Their position in the early history of America —when she was struggling from the darkness of foreign political government, reigned over on one hand by royal governors, and on the other by proprietary rights, still more arrogant and grinding—was one of greatest importance, since on their good or evil will depended the life or death of the many small settlements in New England and the Southern States, while they were regarded as invaluable factors and agents in the ever-increasing differences between the French occupation of Canada and the English pretensions thereto.

We have but lately read of the last act of Vandalism perpetrated by the Republican Government of France, the demolition of the Expiatory Chapel on the Boulevard Haussmann, within whose sacred precincts those loyal to the old Bourbon cause were wont to repair to show their loyalty to that most unfortunate queen, Marie Antoinette.

Very few who have visited that little shrine, and read the touching words on the two monuments erected to Louis XVI. and his Queen, but will hear with regret of its speedy destruction; hitherto it has been held in some manner sacred, and however doubtful may have been the memorials treasured there, it was at least an expression of melancholy justice, and formed a *rendezvous* for all who were left of the old Royalist party. But even the most loyal-hearted of them all, who laid their lilies on the tombs of the son of St. Louis and his beautiful wife, or the most thoroughgoing fanatic in a dead cause, would scarcely see the connection between the little Expiatory Chapel and the wide, rolling prairies of the great West, or between the unfortunate, sad Queen and the savage Red Indian of America. And yet, so strange are the romances of history that the very closest of all ties is said to have united these two extremes, and that the treasure which the Duc de Provence, the Committee of Safety, and the jailers of the Temple guarded so carelessly, the Iroquois and Oneida tribes of the

American Indians protected with fidelity and affection.

When Robespierre died by the sharp knife of his own "Jeanne Marie," and the fury of the Revolutionary government came to an end, having glutted itself in the blood of its King and Queen and highest *noblesse*, there still remained one poor little royal prisoner to whom the opening of all prison doors made small difference. "The little Capet," so called by the Assembly, or Louis XVII., King of France and Navarre, was still a State prisoner in one of the strong towers that formed the dreary precincts of the Temple. Since his captivity he had lost father, mother, and aunt, and there remained to him, after the death of the saintly Madame Elizabeth, only his sister, who was separated from him, and his two uncles, the Ducs de Provence and D'Artois. No figure in all history stands

LOUIS XVII.
From the picture in the Bryan Gallery, New York

forth more pathetically than that of the little Dauphin, who had been the darling of his parents, the hope of the Bourbon dynasty, and whose final destination is wrapped in so much mystery.

There was one little spot of ground in the Tuileries gardens that used to speak most eloquently of him; that one little garden-bed, where, after the removal of the royal family from Versailles, he used to cultivate his flowers, working assiduously day by day to have his morning nosegay as a greeting for his mother. This same little historic plot became the plaything of the little Roi de Rome, under Napoleon's reign, while Charles X. consecrated it to the use of the little Duc de Burgundy, and Louis Philippe gave it to the Count de Paris, while doubtless the late Prince Imperial planted his violets in the self-same spot, and reviewed his boy soldiers where once the little Capet had drilled his company of "Royal Dauphins."

It is not within the scope of this slight sketch to enter upon the different causes which ended in the Revolution of 1793; it is an epoch regarding which so much has been written that no recapitulation is necessary to place its prominent features before the reader. Let us then presuppose a knowledge of all such facts, and step at once into the mysterious entourage that from the fall of Robespierre surrounded the life of the young king, Louis XVII.

His uncle, the Duc de Provence, an unscrupulous and ambitious man, had declared himself Regent in behalf of the boy king, on the death of Louis XVI., whom, as Lamartine says, "he loved as much as it was possible for him to love any one ranking above him." But this usurpation of power was not solely in the interests of his nephew; the Duc de Provence, even before the death of his brother, was intriguing to obtain at least the Regency in case of Louis XVI.'s abdication, if not mounting to the throne by the voice of the people, whose "king" he hoped to become. The famous "Fitzjames" letters show how the wind blew, and how he intended to strike at the Queen's honour, written, as they presumably were, by him. In that of May 13th, 1787, dated from Versailles and signed Louis Stanislaus Xavier, he says, "Here is, my dear Duke, the Assembly of Notables drawing to its close, and yet the great question has not been touched upon. You cannot doubt that the Notables will not hesitate to believe, from the documents which you sent them, more than six weeks ago, that the King's children are not his own. The fact in question once averred, it is easy to infer the consequences. The Parliament which dislikes the Queen will not make any great difficulty, but if it should have the fancy to raise any, we have the means of bringing it to reason. In short, we must attempt the blow."

Some five or six years later he writes to the Count d'Artois: "It is done, my brother,—*the blow is struck*. I hold in my hand the official news of the death of the unfortunate Louis XVI. I am informed also that his son is dying. You will not forget how useful to the State their deaths will be, and remember that the Grand Prior, your son, is, after me, the hope and heir to the monarchy."

Not much of brotherly love is to be found in these two letters, while if the former be taken in connection with the Duc's appearance at the Assembly of Notables in 1787 (the same year as the date of the "Fitzjames" letter), for the first time publicly in the character of reformer, throwing all his weight against the aristocracy, and allying himself with the masses as the champion of sweeping constitutional amendment, it will not be difficult to accept Lamartine's digest of his political schemes, converging to but one end—his own ascendency to the throne of his brother. "All reform which extended to his own dynasty appeared to him sacrilegious. He foresaw a revolution ... and believed that France, reconstructed on a new monarchical plan, would take refuge under his own government." That he played fast and loose with each faction in turn, to suit his own plans, is evidenced by his treatment of Charette, whom he cajoled as the head of a dangerous party—whose object was to wrest the Dauphin from prison, and, proclaiming him king, arouse the country in his cause—even while he fooled the Convention by his plausible acquiescence in their plans. One fact in all the turmoil of that time stands prominently forward: neither party—that of the self-styled Regent, nor that of the Convention—desired to see the little king proclaimed sovereign of France; while any plan that encompassed his removal would be quietly winked at, and no questions asked as to the manner of that removal. The conversation that took place between the deputation of the Committee of General Safety and Simon, the Dauphin's jailer, exemplifies the real feelings of both parties: "Citizens, what is to be done with this young wolf? He is insolent. I will tame him; but what, after all, is desired? Carry him away?" "No." "Kill him?" "No." "Poison him?" "No." "What then?" "*Get rid of him.*"

Six months of solitary confinement followed the departure of Simon before another guardian was appointed for the "little Capet," in the person of Laurent, a Republican soldier with a most kindly heart. He at once visited the Temple, and asked for the rooms of the little prisoner. When the door was forced they found him lying on his bed worn to a skeleton, with tumours at his elbows, knees, and ankles; his long captivity and the horrible treatment to which he had been subjected had culminated in a state of imbecility and physical prostration. "His open eyes had no expression; their colour had changed; he had the look, not of a fool, but of an idiot."

The next act in the drama was Laurent's petition for a colleague and the appointment of Gomin; and here is to be seen the hand of the Regent, who procured this position for Gomin through his friend the Marquis de Fénouil, who, though a Republican outwardly, was in his heart devoted to the Regent's cause; and henceforward whatever took place in the Temple was accomplished with the knowledge and sanction of the Duc de Provence. Matters had now reached such a crisis that to the two political factions—that of the Republican party in power, and the Regent's party intriguing for power—the death of the young king offered the only peaceable solution of all difficulties; and if this result did not come to pass in the due course of nature, there were those who would not hesitate to proclaim the event even at the risk of losing their heads should their plans be discovered and frustrated by the only loyal party, that of Charette at the head of his Vendean troops.

On the 26th of February, 1794, Laurent and Gomin reported to the Committee of General Safety on the precarious state of their little prisoner's health. When asked the nature of his condition, they replied that "the little Capet had tumours on all the articulations, and particularly at the knees, and that it was *impossible to obtain from him a single word.*" Lamartine gives a touching picture of the Dauphin as he was found by the Committee who visited him. "The Prince was sitting before a little square table on which were scattered some playing cards, some bent into the form of boxes and little chests, others piled up in castles. He was amusing himself with these cards when we entered, but did not give up his play. He was dressed in a soldier's jacket of slate-coloured cloth, his head was bare."

Harmand, one of the deputies, spoke to him, and endeavoured in many ways to make him speak, but could get no response in words; the mechanical movement of his limbs was the only indication of sense he showed during the interview. The deputies questioned his attendants as to the reason of this "obstinate silence," and were assured by them that ever since the fatal day when the monstrous deposition against his mother had been forced from him, the poor child had ceased to speak,—"remorse had prostrated his understanding."

It is well to bear in mind this account of Lamartine's, as Beauchesne, the friend of Louis Philippe, in his account of the last days of the young king Louis XVII., written some fifty or sixty years after the events which he depicts with so lively and detailed a pencil, omits the last sentence, placing three stars in its place.

In the following year Laurent resigned his position, and the vacancy was filled by the appointment of Etienne Lasnè, who had been a soldier in the Garde Française, and was an instrument of the Republican faction, as Gomin was a creature of the Marquis de Fénouil. On the arrival of Lasnè several important changes took place in the care of the young king; the espionage over him was much relaxed, and the order for two guards to be always with him was disregarded, Gomin and Lasnè taking turns in sitting with him alone; while the locks and keys of the doors in his apartment were oiled and made to work noiselessly. Evidently some plan was on foot in which both Lasnè and Gomin were concerned, and which was to cut the Gordian knot of the living presence of Louis XVII., and free both political parties from the onerousness of their position.

In the meantime the Royalist cause had never looked so prosperous. Thiers tells us how the cry for the restoration was universal, until matters assumed so grave an aspect that the Government came to terms with Charette, promising to deliver the young king into his hands in the following June. In all of these projects the Regent seemed to concur, though in reality he kept his agents ready to act as he saw fit when the moment came that he found his nephew in the way of his own accession to the throne.

The 13th of June was rapidly approaching, the day on which the Convention had agreed to deliver the royal prisoners, the Dauphin and his sister Madame Royal, to the care of Charette; therefore whatever plans were laid to the contrary had to be worked out and completed by the end of May. The Marquis de Fénouil was well acquainted, working as he did with the Government, with all that took place in the Temple, and through his creatures Gomin and Lasnè expected to outwit both the Vendeans and the Convention.

In the beginning of May the bulletin in the

Register of the Temple ran as follows: "The little Capet is indisposed;" the next day, "The little Capet is dangerously ill, and there is fear of his death." The result of these informal bulletins was the visit of Desault, the celebrated physician, who was authorised by the Convention to attend him, and who first visited him on the 6th. His report of the "dangerous illness" was not calculated to please the Regent's faction, as he pronounced the swellings at the knees and wrists not to be of a scrofulous nature, but due to starvation and ill-usage; he ordered the simplest remedies, and according to the Duchesse D'Angoulême, undertook to cure him. Throughout all the long examination, however, the child preserved the same unbroken silence.

Up to the end of May Desault visited him daily, and towards the last the Dauphin showed a hesitating and timid interest in him. On the

30th of May the good doctor made his last visit, though neither he nor the child supposed it to be so.

The terribly sudden death of Desault was proclaimed on the 1st of June; a death so sudden and so unexpected as to throw all Paris into excitement, and which his pupil, M. Abeillé, did not hesitate to declare was due to poison.

Here then was removed in a remarkable manner, at a remarkable time, the only person of distinction and position who had it in his power to discover the plots of the Duc de Provence, and through whose devotion doubtless the Dauphin would soon have obtained his liberty.

On the morning of the 31st of May the Acting Commissary arrived at the Temple, and said he would wait for the doctor in the prisoner's apartment, and was allowed to do so and to remain alone with the child, Gomin and

Lasnè permitting this flagrant breach of rule. The Commissary was none other than Bellanger, an artist, whose patron was the Regent, and for whose good-will he was ready to act as he might be directed. Several days passed, during each of which he was a constant visitor, going and coming as he pleased, without regard to hours or rules, and having ample opportunity to carry out any plan of abduction and secretion that might be devised. It was not until the 5th of June that another doctor was appointed,—an unpardonable delay if the Dauphin was so seriously ill as was reported. M. Pellatin, the new physician, unlike M. Desault, had never seen the young Prince, while the former doctor had frequently visited him in happier days; consequently, had any substitute been introduced in the place of the Dauphin, M. Pellatin would not have been able to detect the fraud. On his appointment, however, he asked for further help, as he found his patient in "so sad a state he could not bear alone the responsibility of his position." A very different statement from Desault's, who had never once pronounced the child in danger. And here may well be introduced the evidence given in Ireland's "France" (1822), showing the conviction of one class of society as to the authenticity of the child then in the Temple, who was introduced to Pellatin as the Dauphin:—

"My authority for the following narrative is a very respectable tradesman who has heard his father, to whom the circumstances occurred, repeat it in society fifty times: 'As I was then a resident in that quarter of Paris where the Temple was situated, in my capacity as a National Guard, it became my turn to attend there as sentry, when having seen the Dauphin about six months before, and being anxious to behold him again prior to his death, as the current report was his being in a dangerous state, I applied to the jailer to know whether I might be permitted to occupy the post of the Guard destined to keep watch over the Dauphin's apartment. To this request he acceded with one proviso. I was not to exchange a single syllable with Citizen Capet, as the infringement of such order would be attended by the loss of my head. I promised, and immediately entered upon my duty. In the room there were three common chairs, a table, and a low bedstead whereon the Dauphin was lying; but from the position of the bedclothes I could not perceive his countenance. I remained thus for the space of an hour, only observing at intervals a motion beneath the bed-covering. At length, however, he pushed away the sheet from his head, when I was enabled to consider a countenance squalid in the extreme, partially covered with blotches. As he perceived in me a stranger, he inquired in a faint voice who I was; but the peremptory order received and the heavy price set upon a breach of my faith sealed my lips. At this he appeared displeased, and after turning about, I beheld his body rise until he sat upright in the bed, when nothing could exceed my astonishment on viewing a figure much taller from the head to the bottom of the back than the Dauphin could possibly have displayed. My wonder, however, increased on beholding him thrust his legs from beneath the covering, from which I was enabled to form an estimate of the height of the figure before me if standing erect; when I felt a conviction that no such change could have taken place in the growth of a youth in a half year—in short, a more pitiable object never met the human sight, whoever it may have been, for as to the Dauphin, *I am fully convinced it was not him.*' On explaining to the jailer his doubt as to the identity of the prisoner with Louis XVII., adding as a proof his having seen the Dauphin six months previous, and the absolute impossibility of any such extraordinary growth having taken place in so short a time, he was answered, ' Sick children, citizen, will sometimes shoot up very fast ; go home and keep a still tongue in your mouth, lest you should grow shorter by a head.' "

Beauchesne in his history leaves out this piece of evidence, and proceeds to give the last hours of the Dauphin as described by Gomin and Lasnè, who, though solemnly assuring the Commissioners and Desault only ten days previous that the little Capet refused to utter a word and remained absolutely dumb, now describe him as lively in conversation and full of the most moral and edifying death-bed platitudes,— a change as impossible in mental growth as was that found by the guard in his physical stature. According to Lasnè, the Prince died at two hours and a quarter after mid-day, on the 8th of June; but neither he nor Gomin made any haste to inform the Convention of this most important fact, and when Gomin did arrive at the Tuileries he found the session over for the day, and was in consequence unable to lay his report before the Government, but meeting one of the members he told him, and was requested to "*keep the secret until to-morrow.*" The next day the *procès verbal* was made out, and curiously enough the Committee thought best to assert that they received the information at a quarter past two the day before, when in fact Gomin had not then left the Temple, and Lasnè had not reported the death to his companions, and the Committee had already dispersed. This same *procès verbal* is not dated with the year,—a strange oversight in so important a document; in fact, it displays throughout a carelessness that would scarcely have been permitted had the real Dauphin died as reported on the 8th of June.

On that day, however, instead of listening to Gomin's report of the last affecting moments of Louis XVII., the Committee were engaged upon a far more important business,—that of preparing and issuing orders to all the heads of police in and about Paris for the careful searching of all post carriages leaving the city, as it was believed the Dauphin would be carried off from the Temple in some such manner.

Quoting from the London *Atlas*, we find this comment :—" The great fact of the escape of the

Dauphin from the Temple is well established by the archives of the police, where is still preserved the order sent out to the departments to arrest on every highroad in France any travellers bearing with them a child of about eight years, as there had been an escape of Royalists from the Temple. The order bears date June 8th, 1795." Of the action taken upon this order we need only mention the arrest of M. Guérwière, who was travelling in the carriage of the Prince de Condé, "under the suspicion that he, then a child of ten years, was the Dauphin."

It would be impossible to enter into all the mass of evidence in proof of the abduction of the Prince by agents acting, doubtless, under the ægis of the Duc de Provence. He had the opportunity and the tools to work with; was it likely that he, with his unscrupulous ambitious character, would let slip such a chance of relieving both parties and salving his own conscience? The Dauphin removed out of the country, a false prince introduced in his place, whose death would satisfy the demands and scruples of the Government, would leave him free to carry out his own plans for self-aggrandisement, while the sin of murder would not rest upon his soul; since he had secret emissaries who could always communicate with him and his royal nephew, whose unhappy state of mind rendered him unfit for any position of responsibility, but whose lawful claims to the throne could not be set aside so long as he was known to be alive.

The subsequent conduct of Loüis XVIII. goes to prove this, as neither at the time of his accession nor during any part of his reign did he make any public acknowledgment of the absolute death of his nephew, or erect any monument to his memory, or seek out his grave; while on the other hand he made great public exertions to find the remains of his brother, Louis XVI., and Marie Antoinette, and erected to their memories monuments of esteem and affection.

After the drama of the Hundred Days in 1815 —when all Europe was convulsed at the apparent revivification of Napoleon's despotism, when the scarcely acclimatised king, Louis XVIII., and his family were again obliged to fly, and during which the Duchesse D'Angoulême displayed such courageous intrepidity as to draw from Bonaparte the remark that "she was the only man of her family," and which ended in the triumphal re-entry of the king, and the banishment from France, for ever, of the Corsican Emperor —public opinion, which had been too engrossed with the exciting topics of the immediate present to bestow any sentiment upon the past, demanded from Louis XVIII. some expression of regret and esteem in memory of his royal nephew, to whom rightfully belonged the throne of France.

This public sentiment went so far as to cause the passing of a decree in both Chambers, that a monument should be erected, at the public expense, to Louis XVII. The King, with his usual plasticity, agreed cordially to the scheme, and threw so much apparent affection into it as to delegate Lemot to execute the monument, which was to be placed in the Madeleine, in whose cemetery the bodies of his unfortunate relatives, Louis XVI. and Marie Antoinette, and their faithful Swiss Guards had been thrown. He also employed M. Belloc to draw up a suitable epitaph. But here all action ended; the monument was never erected, one royal pretext after another being given for the delay, and the pompous Latin eulogy on the child-king remained among the State papers as a curiosity only. It ran as follows :—

TO THE MEMORY

OF LOUIS XVII.,

WHOM

FROM HIS SACRED PARENTS

SEPARATED BY A MOURNFUL FATE,

AND STRICKEN WITH EVERY SORROW,

ON THE VERY THRESHOLD OF LIFE, DEATH REMOVED

ON THE 8TH DAY OF JUNE, 1795.

HE LIVED 10 YEARS, 2 MONTHS, 10 DAYS.

LOUIS XVIII.

HATH ERECTED THIS

TO HIS NEPHEW MOST LOVELY,

AND BEYOND THE MEASURE OF HIS AGE RELIGIOUS.

HAIL, INNOCENT SOUL,

WHO, LIKE A GLITTERING STAR OF FRANCE,

WALKEST IN THE BLESSED SKIES;

AUSPICIOUSLY, THIS COUNTRY AND THE HOUSE

OF BOURBON, WITH PLACID EYE BEHOLD.

The Duc de Provence could not change his nature, though he became King of France, and he had not the courage to publicly put forward so bold a falsehood. There were others beside himself concerned in the abduction of the Dauphin, and he could have no surety that, were he to authoritatively assert the young king's death, they would not come forward to prove his being alive, and show the Regent's hand in the matter. The Duchesse D'Angoulême, who wept so passionately over the murdered body of her cousin, the Duc D'Enghien, and who attended the obsequies held over his remains at the Madeleine, was not likely to permit the evident sarcasm implied in the bald honour of a monumental tomb to her brother's memory.

If the child who did die in the Temple was in truth the Dauphin, why, since his place of burial in the cemetery of St. Marguerite was well known, did not Louis XVIII. exhume the body and have it re-interred at the same time, and with the same pomp, as was bestowed upon the very uncertain remains of the young king's unfortunate parents? His sister, while bowing to the superior will of her uncle, could not have sanctioned such a direct imposition as a public interment of the body of the poor Temple victim would have countenanced.

In consulting the testimony of M. Labreli Fontaine, who was librarian to the Duchesse D'Orleans, we find that "the first article of the secret treaty of Paris, 1814, explains the manner in which the powers of Europe had permitted the Duc de Provence to occupy the throne of France. Although the high contracting powers, the allied sovereigns, have no certain evidence of the death of the son of Louis XVI., the state of Europe and its political interests require that they should place at the head of the government in France Louis

Xavier, Count de Provence, ostensibly with the title of king; but being, in fact, considered in their secret transactions only as regent of the kingdom for the two years next ensuing, reserving to themselves during that period to obtain every possible certainty concerning a fact which must ultimately determine who shall be the sovereign of France."

And again, M. Bourbon le Blanc published the attestation of M. Pegold, notary of Crossen, in which he affirmed that "there was not a sovereign in Europe who did not in 1818 receive letters from him on the subject," namely, the abduction of the Dauphin from the Temple.

It is, then, a granted hypothesis that the young king Louis XVII. did not die in the Temple as reported. The next question that naturally arises is as to the possible place of his banishment, and where and how he grew up, and why his claims were never brought forward and established. Now, putting aside the pretensions of Naundorff and Richemont,—which were utterly confounded and discredited by the Duchesse D'Angoulême,—we still have evidence that she fully believed her brother to be alive, and admitted this, while she hinted at his whereabouts ; but her devotion to her uncle, Louis XVIII., was of such a nature, and her memory of the unfortunate mental condition of the Dauphin so sad, she did not deem it expedient to institute any official inquiries.

Bearing in mind all the extraordinary facts and circumstances that surround the fate of Louis XVII., it will, notwithstanding, doubtless give rise to a smile of incredulity when the theory is brought forward that Louis XVII., King of France, was carried to America, with the consent and co-operation of the Regent, and deposited with the Indians of the Iroquois tribe ; that with them he grew into youthhood, and that as their friend and missionary he lived and died, though knowing his claims to the throne of France to be far more substantial and credible than any that had been put forth.

Yet such was and is the belief in many thinking minds, and so complete was the circumstantial evidence that many of the most prominent men of America, forty odd years ago, publicly acknowledged this conviction.

Among these were the late Bishop of New York, Dr. Potter; the Hon. Hamilton Fisk; the Rev. F. L. Hawkes, D.D., LL.D.; the Bishop of California, Dr. W. Ingraham Kip; the Hon. John Jay, late Minister to Vienna; Chevalier Fagnani; Mr. A. Fleming,* and the Rev. J. H. Hanson, a great grandson of Oliver Goldsmith.

---

* Mr. Fleming was a direct descendant of that family, one of whose members, Mary Fleming, was the devoted friend and Maid of Honour to Mary Queen of Scots.

And now the scene changes, and we must step backward over a century to gather up one link in the strange chain of events which unites the fortunes of the Dauphin of France with those of the Red Man of North America. In the year 1704 there occurred at Deerfield, Massachusetts, one of those terrible incursions of the Indians which were the terror of the new country. Lord Cornbury—detested alike for his vices and his eccentricities, the lightest of which was his habit of appearing in public dressed as a woman, and giving as his reason that since his Royal Queen and cousin was a woman, it behoved her representatives to adopt the habiliments of her sex—was then Governor of New York, and though he sent intelligence of a probable rising of the St. François Indians to the Governor of Massachusetts in 1703, it was not until the early part of the new year that it actually took place.

There lived in Deerfield at that time the Rev. John Williams and his family. He was the pastor of the village, and a man of no ordinary attainments. In 1697, when a similar attack had been made, he, at the head of his flock, had repulsed and routed the enemy; but, with their usual long patience, the St. François' waited for, and accomplished their revenge. On the 28th of February, 1704, the Rev. Mr. Williams retired to rest as usual without any premonition of danger, but at daybreak the village was attacked, and the noise of axes and hammers sounding a *reveillé* was the first notification of alarm. The Indians entered Mr. Williams' house, and before his eyes murdered two of his children, while he and his wife and their remaining little ones were taken prisoners. Through deep snow they made their weary way; in front of them stretched three hundred miles to be traversed before they reached the home of the St. François, who were followers of the French Jesuits. After a very rapid journey, during which Mrs. Williams was murdered, they arrived at Montreal; and here his little daughter, Eunice, was adopted by the Jesuit Mission, and baptized in the Catholic faith. This was a terrible blow to the Puritan minister, —far worse than his compulsory attendance at Mass.

The little Eunice, however, fell in love with her new friends, and not only adopted the religion of her dusky companions, but their language and customs as well, and later on became a thorough Indian by marrying a young native of the name of Turoges, which is considered to be a corruption of De Rogers.

She completely forgot her mother tongue, and could never be got to renounce any of the habits of savage life. She was, however, never forgotten in her New England village, where, after her father's return, her strange fate was the cause of many prayer-meetings, and her re-conversion the source of much earnest prayer. Before her father's death in 1729 she once visited Deerfield, dressed in her blanket and wampum, and though she consented to attend "meeting" in civilized attire, she got rid of it as soon as possible, and returned to the life of her choice.

She had three children, a son and two daughters. Her son, John De Rogers, was killed at Lake George in 1758; her daughter Catharine married an Indian called Rice, and Mary married an English physician, who though named Williams was no relation. They had one son, Thomas Williams, or Tehorakwaneken, who in his turn married an Indian named Mary Ann Konwatewenteta, in January 1799.

Throughout the Revolution Thomas Williams fought on the British side, and rendered good service to General Waterbury and Burgoyne. He had eight children, who were all baptized Catholics at the Mission of Caughnawaga. The habits of Thomas Williams were known to be peculiar and secretive, and he was often absent from his family for long periods without thinking it necessary to make any explanation. On returning from one of these absences he brought with him a young boy of about eight or nine years old; a fair, delicate child, whose features were refined and sensitive, though his mind was seemingly vacant and imbecile.

And now to return to civilization. In 1795 there came to Albany, the capital of New York State, and a city of much importance and wealth, four strangers who had come direct from France. At that time many refugees sought protection in America, but these persons attracted special attention. They gave their name as De Jardin, and the party consisted of a lady, a gentleman, and two children, the eldest of whom was a girl called Louise, the other a little boy named Louis. The lady, though bearing the same name as the gentleman, was never considered to be his wife in any respect; he, indeed, was evidently her inferior, and never obtruded his presence in any way. The children under their care were guarded with much mystery, and were never allowed to be seen in public, especially the boy, who was only visited by one or two ladies and children, and who appeared to be very quiet and deficient for one of his age. Madame De Jardin possessed several things that had belonged to Louis XVI. and Marie Antoinette. She stated frankly that she had been a maid-of-honour to the unfortunate Queen, and was separated from her before her imprisonment in the Temple; she spoke with much emotion, and burst into tears at the name of the Queen. The children were spoken of at the time as not being those of Madame De Jardin, and the boy at least was regarded as one of the royal family of France.

Mrs. Dudley, a member of Governor Seymour's family, speaks of them in a letter dated 1853 as follows:—

"Among the reminiscences of early days I have always recollected with much interest being taken by my mother to visit a family who arrived here (Albany) in 1795 direct from France. These were a lady and gentleman called De Jardin. They had with them two children, a boy and a girl; the girl was the eldest, the boy about nine or ten; he apparently did not notice us. On my first visit I was much struck with the appearance of the family. A gentleman was in the hall; he showed us into the parlour, but did not enter with us; his dress was very plain, and I never realized how he was connected with the family. We were received with politeness by Madame. After a short interview she took me to a room upstairs, with shelves on one side of the wall, containing a number of handsome books; on a table were jointed cards." (Does not this recall the pathetic figure of the little Dauphin and his playing cards in the Temple?) "I was introduced to Mademoiselle Louise and Monsieur Louis. Mademoiselle and I played together, but Monsieur Louis did not join us; he was dressed in shorts, and amused himself at some distance from us. Madame told my mother she was maid-of-honour to the Queen Marie Antoinette. My mother thought the children were belonging to the Crown. After some time Madame called and said they were obliged to leave us, and had many useful and handsome articles to dispose of, and wished my mother to have the first choice,—a pair of gilt andirons representing lions and a bowl, said to be gold, on which were engraven the arms of France. I have heard it spoken of some time after, and it was said to belong to a gentleman near Albany. The andirons were purchased by General Peter Gansevoort's lady, and are still belonging to a member of that family."

And here let us note the coincidence of the above facts with portions of Naundorff's story. We find the same characters exactly, even to detail; and when coupled with his assertion that the Prince was sent to America, and the correspondence of time, the result is at least startling.

We must now leave Albany, and betake our

selves to the beautiful region about Ticondaroga Lake, and once more we must quote from an eyewitness, who was living as late as 1853, for an account of what took place here the same year of the Jardins' arrival in Albany, 1795. This witness was John Skenondough O'Brien,* an Indian half-breed, the son of an Irishman and an Oneida woman; he was sent to France to be educated, and returned to America during the Revolution. During the hunting season he was often at Lake George, and while at Ticondaroga in 1795, "two Frenchmen, one of them having the appearance of a Roman priest, came there, bringing with them a weak, sickly child,

---

*This Skenondough was a nephew of the old war-chief of that name who dressed Lafayette's wounds at the battle of Brandywine. O'Brien Skenondough was a pensioner of the writer's grandmother when he had reached the great age of one hundred and fifteen.

in a state of mental imbecility. Being acquainted with French, O'Brien conversed with the men, and learned from them that the boy was born in France; he was adopted by an Iroquois chief named Thomas Williams;" and here the narrative is brought down to the time when Williams, returning from one of his long absences, appeared with a foreign child, as unlike an Indian as well could be, and with grave taciturnity bade his wife look after him as one of their own. His name from thenceforward was Eleazar, or Lazu Williams, and from that time Thomas Williams was for many years in receipt of regular moneys which he went to Albany to collect, and which Mr. John Bleeker received from France, to be devoted to the support of Eleazar. Doubtless these transactions were arranged through the Indian, Jacob Vanderheyden, with whom Talleyrand was in correspondence for years. It was this Jacob Vanderheyden who was present at Lake George when the little Eleazar was delivered to the care of the Williams family, and his daughter, Mrs. Catherine Mancius, told the Rev. Mr. Van Rensselear, of Mount Morris, that when Talleyrand visited America he paid her father a visit of considerable length. Williams, however, was as silent about the money as he was about the strange child.

The boy was delicate, refined, sensitive, though so deficient in mind as to be called *l'imbècile;* and while after a few years of free, out-door life his physical health improved, his mental powers, especially that of memory, still remained undeveloped.

He often accompanied his adopted father to Lake George, where the Indian hunting-grounds were occupied year after year by the same tribes; and it was here, some little time after his adoption by the Iroquois, that he fell from a rock near the Old Fort, at the head of the lake, and cut his head severely. On his recovering from the effects of this injury what was his delight to find his poor confused brain becoming clearer, while many things that had seemed only terrible or beautiful dreams assumed definite shapes and reality; his memory, which for so many years had been clouded and obscure, was slowly reawakening.

One of the incidents most vividly impressed upon his mind at this time was the visit of two strange gentlemen to the encampment of Thomas Williams, who took their seats beside him on a log a little distance from his wigwam. Williams called out, " Lazu, this friend of yours wishes to speak to you." As he approached, one of the gentlemen rose and walked off. The one who remained had every indication, in dress, manner, and language, of being a Frenchman; the boy remembered a few words of his native tongue, and so knew that he spoke in French. His hair was powdered; he had on a ruffled shirt, and bore a very splendid appearance. When Eleazar came near he advanced several steps towards him, embraced him most tenderly, and, shedding abundance of tears, called him "*pauvre garçon.*" The Frenchman continued to lament and caress him, speaking rapidly and earnestly, but the lad could not understand him. They came again the next day, and the French gentleman remained several hours; the last thing he did was to take hold of the boy's bare feet and examine them and his ankles closely, when he again shed tears, and on leaving gave him a gold piece.

Thomas Williams, contrary to his usual custom, soon after the visit of the strange gentleman, broke up camp and returned to Chaughnawaga, instead of remaining for the winter at Lake George. Not long after their arrival at home, Eleazar overheard a conversation between his adopted parents, in which Thomas Williams eagerly advocated some project, which the old Indian woman as eagerly discouraged. Thomas Williams, however, persevered; and finally, in answer to his demand, she replied—"If you will do it, you may send away this strange boy; means have been put into your hands for his education, but John I cannot part with."

The boy was excitedly interested in what he heard; but though the memory of it remained with him, he soon forgot to attach any special meaning to it, and before long it faded from his mind.

Very soon after this a great change came into the life of Eleazar. Not long after Thomas

Williams' return to Chaughnawaga, he told young Williams that he and his brother John were to be sent east to be educated. Strangely enough they owed this opportunity to the memory of Eunice Williams, who though long dead had not been forgotten in her native home. The Rev. Nathaniel Ely, who remembered her story, traced out her descendants and offered to bring up two of them " in the fear of the Lord." As we know, Mary Ann Williams was very loth to part with any of her children, and at last only consented to allow John to go if accompanied by " the strange boy, Lazu."

Eleazar was at this time (1800) about fifteen, and John was several years younger.

Their appearance at the New England village of Long Meadow caused great excitement ; they were called the " two Indian youths," though there was something " so singular and mysterious in the difference between them, that those who saw them never forgot it."

Mr. Ely was acquainted with the secret of Eleazar's birth in so far as to know he was French, and of distinguished origin, and throughout all their companionship he treated the young man with extreme respect and courtesy. He was also doubtless aware of the fact that at the time of Eleazar's adoption by the Iroquois, Thomas Williams, two boxes, containing clothing and other personal articles, were left with him. One of these boxes was taken away by one of Thomas Williams' daughters, but the other, in 1854, was still in Montreal, though great efforts were made to keep it concealed. In this box were three medals, or coins—one of gold, one of silver, and one of copper—each bearing the same inscription; they were in fact some of the medals struck at the coronation of Louis XVI. and Marie Antoinette.

The Indians sold the gold and silver ones, but thirty years ago the bronze one was in the possession of the Catholic Bishop of Montreal.

It will at once be seen how easily these important souvenirs could find their way to Montreal, as Chaughnawaga, the winter home of the Williamses, was but a straggling Indian village on the St. Lawrence, opposite Lachine, and within sight of Montreal. Those who placed the strange French boy among the Indians could not have chosen a more secluded spot; while should they at any time wish to re-establish his claim to the throne of France—which the nature of the relics left would imply—they might, through the nearness of Montreal, hope to obtain traces of them, even though the roving and gipsy character of the tribes of that settlement would almost preclude any such result.

A Boston paper of the period thus speaks of

the peculiar difference between the two lads. "John was evidently of Indian birth; he showed no fondness for study, always kept his bows and arrows hid away, and on any excuse would make use of them. Eleazar, though entirely illiterate when he came, soon became fond of his books. John learned little or nothing, and returned home; Eleazar made progress, and remained; he showed none of the traits of the Indian race, and was not regarded as of Indian blood."

To quote again. "John was truly an Indian, with long black hair, his complexion and every feature corresponding with his race; Eleazar had brown hair, hazel eyes, and European features."

Even at this time of his life the boy was asked many questions as to his childhood, for already it was acknowledged that a mystery surrounded him. He spoke once to a playmate of the "painful images before his mind of things in his childhood." His journal for 1800 is most interesting, and shows a mind of no ordinary bent; indeed the facility with which he acquired all knowledge would seem phenomenal had there not been a foundation laid in former years, which, though forgotten and unused for so long, responded at once to culture and learning.*

He remained for five years with Mr. Ely, and improved wonderfully in that short time. His journals, which he kept with faithful regularity, show his mental development, until in 1805 we find them displaying considerable elegance of style. He went to Canada in this year, and at Montreal received such marked attention from distinguished people as to greatly astonish and

---

* This was especially noticeable in his quick attainment of handwriting; in an incredibly short time he wrote a characteristic hand, though when he came to Mr. Ely he was apparently ignorant of the first principles, and kept his journal by signs of his own.

delight him, though he seems to have accepted it all with much dignity, and as one "to the manner born."

In 1806 he had an interview with Bishop Chevreux, then a Catholic priest in Boston, who by his questions and interest in him evidently knew more about his birth and antecedents than he would reveal.

In 1810 he made the acquaintance of Bishop Hobart, who even at that early day was attracted by him, and showed him much attention.

In 1812 he first set out with the full intention of devoting his life as a missionary to the Indians, and as agent to the American Board of Missions he visited Canada. At Sault St. Louis he received a message from the chief of the Iroquois tribe requesting his attendance at their council-house, where he was made a chief of that nation, under the name of Onwarenhiiaki, or "Tree Cutter,"—the same name that had been bestowed upon Sir William Johnson.

During the war of 1812-14 he occupied a most important position between the Indians and the Americans, and rendered such good service in keeping peace between the St. Regis tribe and the two belligerent parties as to be put at the head of the Secret Corps, a position he held with much bravery, discretion, and coolness. His war journal at this time is of exceptional interest, and is the reflex of a mind that was certainly fitted to take foremost rank, and that could not possibly have belonged to an Indian half-breed, whose sole education had been encompassed within five years.

In many delicate positions, that might well have taxed the diplomacy of a political veteran, he displayed unerring judgment and justice, and by his exceptional influence over the Indians settled many questions peaceably that might have been the cause of renewed hostilities.

For his services during the entire war the United States Government paid him £2,000 ($10,000), the whole of which he afterwards spent in building schools and supporting the miserably paid Indian Mission, of which he was the pastor. During this time his religious convictions became identical with the tenets of the Episcopal Church in America, which is the daughter of the Church of England, though not a National Establishment.

An incident occurred at this time that is not without significance. Eleazar was visiting the Rev. Mr. Clowes, of Albany, and on seeing a brilliantly illuminated missal, which lay upon the table, his usually self-possessed and dignified manner deserted him; he became very much agitated, and begged passionately to be given the book;

he was, however, refused, because his manner was so agitated that he was supposed to be suffering from some temporary delusion.

Mr. Hammond, in his most interesting book, gives the following:—" There is now before me an Indian Mass Book in MS., which, from the colour of the paper, the faded writing, and its dilapidated condition, seems at least two centuries old. It was given Mr. Williams (Eleazar) in 1836, by an Indian woman, now dead, who told him that, while in an insane condition, he one day snatched a pen and wrote in it a number of figures and letters. There are on one of the covers, on the inside, in French characters, the numerals from 1 to 30, and from 1 to 19; a letter C. precisely like that element in the handwriting of the Dauphin while under the care of Simon; and in a less distinct form, but still quite legible, the word 'duc' and the letters 'Loui.'"

Another incident is told of him at this time. When looking at some engravings shown him by a friend, one of Simon was exhibited, Professor Day covering the name as he displayed it; immediately Mr. Williams looked at it he exhibited marked signs of distress, and exclaimed in terrified accents, "Good God! I know that face, it has haunted me through life."*

On his return east he began his preparation for the ministry, and in 1815 he went to New York to unfold his plans to the then Bishop, Dr. Hobart. The Bishop received him cordially, and entered with sympathy into all his desires, and after a few weeks sent him among the Indians as a catechist, lay reader, and schoolmaster, and in this humble capacity he laboured

---

* The late United States Minister to Vienna, Mr. John Jay, was present, and heard this remark.

for many years. It is impossible to enter into detail concerning this part of his life, interesting though it is; he remained at his post until 1818, when, his health failing, he went further north into the St. Regis country, and here, it would appear, the first real doubts as to his birth occurred to him. He had a letter of introduction to Mr. Richards, of the Montreal Catholic Seminary, who, on his entering, said, "I believe, Sir, you are the gentleman of whom the Abbé de Calonne, of Three Rivers, has often spoken, as a person whose history was hidden in the womb of mystery in regard to your descent and the cause of your adoption among the Indians—you are a foreigner by birth, and of high family." This so excited Mr. Williams' curiosity, that on his return to Sault St. Louis he examined the parish register of births, and found entered there all of Thomas

Williams' family, but no record of his own name.

In 1819 he was summoned to Washington on a matter of great importance, which was the removal of the New York Indians to the west; and the Government, knowing how great would be the resistance, asked Mr. Williams to act as mediator. It was a position full of difficulties, but these did not deter him; he undertook to negotiate the proposal, which, to his mind, appeared reasonable and advantageous.

This, the first definite move on the part of the United States Government to coerce the Indians from their holdings in New York State, and force them into reservations at the west, opens far too wide a subject to be entered upon here, though it is a question of political ethics which must one day call for liberal discussion and adjustment.

The New York Indians consented to remove their wigwams into the lands formerly occupied by the Menominies and Winnebagoes in the neighbourhood of Green Bay, Wisconsin. Mr. Williams accompanied them to their new home, with the hope that now his dream might be realized, and that by the removal of all the tribes to one common territory, they might be won over to civilization and Christianity by daily intercourse with their white brethren; he hoped also to establish an Indian College, in which the Canadian red-man, as well as those from the States, might receive a liberal university education.

To such a mind as his, kind, frank, generous, the hardships of life in a wilderness, poverty, and isolation held no terrors; while, without his knowing it, he was in this new life to meet the woman of his choice.

In 1823 he married Miss Madeline Jourdan,* a young lady of French and Indian extraction, and of great personal beauty and attraction. It was through this marriage that Mr. Williams came into the possession of between three and four thousand acres of land, a short distance from Green Bay. The manner of Miss Jourdan's (Mrs. Williams) becoming possessed of so fine a property was truly chivalric; among the Menominie tribes, while they held their land in common, certain tracts were set apart as hunting grounds, and held immemorially in particular families.

At the time of the Menominie cession, when a portion of their land was bought by government for the New York Indians, reservation, by express treaty, was made of those hunting grounds for the special benefit of the families holding

---

* Miss Jourdan was a creole, her mother being a half breed Indian, and very handsome.

them ; part of this reservation had for many generations belonged to the Jourdan family, and to avoid any future doubt concerning its title, the chiefs, warriors, and head men of the Menominie nation made over to Mrs. Williams and her heirs for ever a deed of gift of the property, dated August 22nd, 1825, in which they said :—
" For and in consideration of their love and friendship for Magdeline Williams and her heirs, of the Menominie nation, and in consideration of the sum of fifty dollars, they gave, granted, bargained, sold, and quit-claimed the said property."

This document, written in Indian language, and signed by six Menominie chiefs, is one of the most curious and interesting of aboriginal archives.

In the following year Mr. Williams was ordained a deacon by Bishop Hobart, and for ten years he laboured among his Indian flock at Green Bay, and then, though obliged to resign his position, he in after years returned to St. Regis and his dusky flock.

It was during his residence at Oneida, 1819-20, that Mr. Williams was visited by Le Ray Chaumont, who made as his excuse his desire to enquire after a Colonel De la Ferrière, who had left France during the Revolution, and who had married an Indian woman of Oneida. In conversation Le Ray remarked that "Le Ferrière had been a great sufferer for the royal cause, that the king's family had been widely scattered, but that notwithstanding all the misfortunes of De Ferrière, he was no greater sufferer than a member of the royal family, whom both Colonel De Ferrière and he believed to be in this country." A belief which Citizen Genet, the French Ambassador, evidently shared, as he stated positively in New York, at the house of Dr. Hossack, before several people, that

Louis XVII. had not died. "Gentlemen," he said, "the Dauphin of France *is not dead, but was brought to America*,"—adding that Le Ray Chaumont knew all about it.*

It will be remembered that it was this M. Genet who had agreed, before Louis XVI.'s death, to bring the royal children to America, when he came as ambassador. A carriage was provided with a false back, in which they were to make their escape, but on the eve of departure the mob seized the carriage and destroyed it.

Le Ray Chaumont was in correspondence with Count Real and Count Jean d'Angley at the time when the existence of the Dauphin was being much discussed in Paris.

---

* It was at this gathering that Talleyrand, who was present, spoke to Dr. Francis, and gave him such information as to leave no doubt in his mind, that Talleyrand believed the Dauphin to be alive, and in America.

De Ferrière went to Paris in 1817, taking several Indians with him, but before he left he went to see Mr. Williams, and obtained from him his signature to some legal documents. It was told afterwards, by one of the Indians, that while they were in Paris, Colonel De Ferrière received great attention, and that he, the Indian, was taken to see some person of great distinction who asked him who was their religious teacher in Oneida. He answered, Eleazar Williams. He was again asked very particularly if he was sure Eleazar Williams was there, and he replied yes; thereupon he was dismissed, but Colonel De Ferrière returned to Oneida a rich man, whereas he left a poor one.

The Rev. Mr. Hanson, of New York, reports a conversation which he held with Mr. Williams in 1851, and which, though rather antedating the subject, it is advisable to insert at this point.

Mr. Hanson had become interested in Mr. Williams first through his brave missionary work, and secondly, in seeing a paragraph in the *New York Courier and Enquirer* containing the announcement that there were grave reasons for supposing him to be the son of Louis XVI. Mr. Hanson says frankly that at first this struck him as only a sensational rumour, and he did not then know Mr. Williams was working with the St. Regis tribes, but supposed him still to be at Green Bay. Later a friend told him that Mr. Williams had left the Green Bay Indians, and was among the St. Regis, not far from Mr. Hanson's home in Waddington. It was accident, however, that brought about an interview between them. Mr. Hanson, on leaving St. Lawrence county, took the train at Ogdensburgh for New York, and from this point let his own account speak :—

" Upon entering the cars, I observed a somewhat

stout old gentleman, talking to two Indians in their own language, in a very animated manner, and was much interested in watching the varied play of their and his countenances. It occurred to me that it was Mr. Williams, and on the conductor confirming my supposition I introduced myself to him. He was going to Burlington, Vermont, and from thence to Boston; and as our route lay down Champlain, we took the steamer together. I was perfectly familiar with the Indian lineaments and characteristics, and I was not sorry to have so good an opportunity of comparing his appearance with his reputed countrymen; he presented in every respect the marks of a different race."

In the course of conversation Mr. Hanson spoke of the strong feeling shown by Mr. Williams' friends, that his identity might be firmly established, and then questioned him on several points. Mr. Williams replied frankly and modestly, though he admitted that the subject was painful to him, and he could not speak upon it unmoved. In regard to his remembering anything connected with his childhood, he said :—

" There lies the mystery of my life. I know nothing about my infancy. Everything that occurred to me then is blotted out, entirely erased, irrevocably gone. You must imagine a child, who, as far as he knows anything, was an idiot, destitute even of consciousness that can be remembered, until that period. He was bathing on Lake George, among a group of Indian boys. He clambered with the fearlessness of idiocy to the top of a high rock. He plunged down, head foremost, into the water. He was taken up insensible, and laid in an Indian hut. He was brought to life. There was the blue sky, there were the mountains, there were the waters. That was the first I knew of life."

A little later, after mentioning several remarkable coincidences, he said :—"And now comes in evidence of a different description. A French gentleman hearing my story, bought a printed account of the captivity of the Dauphin, and read me a note in which it was stated that Simon the jailer, having become incensed with the Prince for some childish offence, took a towel which was hanging on a nail, and in snatching it hastily drew out the nail with it, and inflicted two blows upon his face, one over the left eye, and the other on the right side of the nose. 'And now,' said he, 'let me look at your face.' When he did so, and saw the scars on the spots indicated in the memoirs, he exclaimed, '*Mon Dieu!* what proof do I want more?'

"But that is not all; in the same memoirs it is said that the Dauphin died of scrofula, and the disease was on his knees. My knees are eaten up with scrofula, and there are no other scrofulous marks on my body. You can yourself remark the alleged resemblance between me and Louis XVIII., and the Bourbon family in general. I remember a gentleman put his hand over the name attached to a picture of Louis XVIII., and asked whose portrait it was. 'That of Mr. Williams,' was the reply. 'I have somewhat of a curiosity in my valise,' he continued, 'and will show it to you; it is a dress of Marie Antoinette's; it was given me by a person who bought it in France, and who, hearing my story, considered me the rightful owner, and made me a present of it.'

"The dress itself was of very rich brocade, somewhat faded. It had been taken apart, and the pieces consisted of a skirt, stomacher, back piece, and a train some three or four yards long. The *ceinture* of the bodice was very slender. Fortunately for the authenticity of this relic, the note of presentation is still preserved, and runs as follows :—' Presented to the Rev. Eleazar Williams, with the respectful regards of Mrs. Edward Clarke, of Northampton. Being in England some years since, she had an opportunity there of purchasing this dress, once worn by the Queen Marie Antoinette of France. It had been bought at the Court by a gentleman attached to the Embassy. Mrs. Clarke was informed that the dresses once worn by the Queen were afterwards distributed among the ladies of the Court, who would sometimes dispose of them in this manner at auction.

"'ROUND HILL, NORTHAMPTON,
"'*January* 3rd, 1851.'"

Mr. Hanson draws a lifelike portrait of Mr.

Williams, which must at once strike the reader by its Bourbonic type :—" His complexion is rather dark, like that of one who had become bronzed by living much in the open air; his features are rather heavily moulded, and strongly characterized by the full, protuberant Austrian lips ; his head is well formed, and sits proudly on his shoulders ; his eyes are dark, but not black ; his hair may be called black, is rich and glossy, and interspersed with grey ; his eyebrows are full, and of the same colour (upon the left is a scar) ; his beard is heavy ; his nose aquiline, the nostril large and finely cut. His temperament is genial, with a dash of vivacity in his manners, and he inclines to *embonpoint*, which is the characteristic of the Bourbon family."

The truth of these peculiar traits was startlingly brought out in a daguerreotype taken of Mr. Williams, wearing across his black coat, from shoulder to shoulder, the broad ribbon of the royal order of France, and through the intensified lights and shadows of the daguerre his marked and expressive face was fully limned, and he looked indeed every inch a king.

In 1841 the Prince de Joinville visited America, and on arriving in New York, asked immediately whether there was a person known as Eleazar Williams among the Indians at the north. He was told that there was such a person, and that he was a missionary at Green Bay, but that Mr. Thomas Ludlow Ogden, of New York, could give him more particulars. He applied to Mr. Ogden, and that gentleman wrote to Mr. Williams, stating the Prince's desire to meet him. It was not, however, until October that the interview took place, and then the Prince had made his way to Lake Michigan, asking at various points for particulars of Mr. Williams.

After the steamer left Mackinac with both the Prince de Joinville and Mr.. Williams on board, the former, who had had Mr. Williams pointed out to him on the wharf, sent a message to him, requesting an interview. When Mr. Williams approached him the Prince started visibly, and showed much agitation. He took Mr. Williams respectfully by the hand, and paid him such marked attention as to astonish not only the other passengers, but his own retinue.

And here let us quote verbatim from Mr. Williams' journal. We find the following under the date of "October 18th, Monday.—I was introduced to a gentleman who was the Prince de Joinville. I was struck at the manner of his salutation. He appeared to be surprised and amazed as he grasped my hand in both of his, which was accompanied by strong and cheering gratulations of his having had an opportunity to meet me, and that upon the surface of one of the inland seas in the Western world. 'Amazing sight!' he continued; 'it is what I have wished to see for this long time. I trust I shall not be intruding too much on your feelings and patience were I to ask some questions in relation to your past and present life among the Indians.' His eyes were intently fixed upon me, eyeing my person from the crown of my head to the soles of my feet."

"October 19th, Tuesday.—This morning the Prince resumed his observations upon the French Revolution. 'Louis XVI.,' he said, 'ought to be placed next to George Washington as a liberator of the American people. . . . My grandfather and father were present when the last struggle took place between the King and the Ministry upon the article of alliance with the United Colonies of America. That day—it was a happy day for Americans, but for the King it was the day of his death.' . . . This afternoon the Prince expressed his wish to take my son with him to France for an education. In connection with this he was informed that we had an infant who had not yet received baptism. He asked to stand as godfather, and would give the name of his mother to the child. But, alas! on my first landing I received the intelligence that the babe was dead. When the news was communicated to the Prince he appeared to sympathize with me, and remarked, taking me by the hand,—' Descendant of a suffering race, may you be supported in this affliction. ' "

It was in the evening of the same day, after they reached Green Bay, that the ever memorable conversation took place between them. To continue Mr. Williams' journal : " At ten o'clock the Prince was pleased to enter into his remarks more particularly upon the family of the unfortunate King, which were at first, with me, somewhat curious and interesting; but as he proceeded with his narration my feelings were greatly excited. . . . The intelligence was not only new, but awful in its nature. To learn for the first time that I was connected by consanguinity with those whose history I had read with so much interest, and for whose sufferings in prison, and the manner of their deaths, I had wept with sympathetic tears!"

The Prince received Mr. Williams at his hotel with only one attendant, and entered at once upon the subject, which he said was of a most serious nature, and though it concerned only themselves, it was of the last importance, and therefore he desired a pledge of secrecy.

After some little demur, Mr. Williams promised conditionally, and the Prince then told him that he was not a native of America, but that he was "of foreign descent, and the son of a king." He then drew an analogy between Mr. Williams' position and that of his father, though, he said, there was this difference,—"he, Louis Philippe, was all along aware of his high birth, while Mr. Williams had no knowledge of his origin."

When Mr. Williams appeared incredulous at such astonishing revelations, and suggested that some mistake had been made as to his identity, the Prince replied that what he said he had ample means of proving. Mr. Williams then asked for the full secret of his birth, and the Prince, in reply, said that in divulging this "it was necessary that a certain process should be gone through, in order to guard the interests of all persons concerned."

He then placed before him a parchment, which he desired Mr. Williams to read and give his answer upon. On the table were pens, ink, paper, and the seal of France, such as was used in Louis XVI.'s reign. The parchment was written in both French and English, and in legal phraseology. It was "a solemn abdication of the Crown of France, in favour of Louis Philippe, by Charles Louis, the son of Louis XVI., who was styled Louis XVII., King of France and Navarre, etc."

The conditions offered in the event of Mr. Williams signing this document were: "A princely establishment to be secured to him either in France or America," and that Louis Philippe would "pledge himself to secure the restoration, or an equivalent, of all the private property of the royal family rightly belonging to him."

Mr. Williams was some hours reading and considering this document; for the first time the secret of his birth was made plain to him, and the humble devoted missionary saw the grand possibilities laid open before him on the one side, if he accepted this agreement, while on the other the old life of poverty, hard work, self-denial, and daily toil was his only prospect. His decision once made, he went to the Prince at once and told him that "he had considered the matter fully in all respects, but that he could not be the instrument of bartering away the rights pertaining to him by birth," and ended by giving the same answer that his enemy and uncle, the Duc de Provence, gave to Napoleon at Warsaw, "Though I am in poverty and exile I will not sacrifice my honour."

In passing judgment on the definite self-sacrifice thus chosen by Mr. Williams, which might well seem an impossible one, we must bear in mind the peculiar characteristics that made up his nature. It will be seen that in this very act he displayed marked family traits; "the generous ardour of his disposition, his religious feelings, his untiring labours for the benefit of others, his absence of pecuniary tact and management, his ignorance even of his own powers, his gentle and forgiving character, and the very want of balance and symmetry in his mind, all agree with the best characteristics of the Bourbons."

The Prince, on hearing Mr. Williams' decision, replied in a loud voice, accusing him of ingratitude to Louis Philippe; to which Mr. Williams replied that since the Prince had put him in the position of a superior he would assume that position, and say frankly that "his indignation was stirred by the memory that one of the family of Orleans had imbrued his hands in his father's blood, and that another now wished to obtain from him an abdication of the throne." The

Prince immediately assumed a respectful attitude, and, after a few moments of silence, they parted for the night; but the next day the subject was again referred to, when Mr. Williams repeated his unalterable decision. The Prince on bidding him good-bye said, " Though we part, I hope we part friends,"—and, in fact, at various times correspondence passed between them, and on one occasion Louis Philippe wrote himself to Mr. Williams, sending to him a package of books as an answer to the petition sent by him at the request of a Catholic Iroquois chief.

The Prince de Joinville had, on his previous visit to America in 1838, gone upon a secret mission into the interior of the State of New York, and on his return to France "inquiries were made of the French vice-consul at Newport concerning two servants of Marie Antoinette, who came to America during the French Revolution."

All these facts and details must be borne in mind on recalling the Prince de Joinville's reply to Mr. Hanson's article in *Putnum's Magazine*, which appeared in 1848—50 under the title of "Have we a Bourbon among us?" and which excited the liveliest interest on both sides of the Atlantic.

The Prince's reply is both too well known and too long to insert; it is sufficient to say that the contradictions it contains are so many proofs of the Prince de Joinville's true feelings and fears upon the subject, though the state of France at that time was inimical to a restoration.

There can be but little doubt that Louis Philippe knew of the existence of the Dauphin and the validity of Mr. Williams' claims.

The citizen king held his throne only on the sufferance of the people, just as he owed it to them; and he supported his sovereignty by dramatic action, such as bringing the ashes of

Napoleon from St. Helena and burying them in France; while he fortified himself with the thought of a *coup d'état* if the Dauphin should return in the person of Mr. Williams, in which he would play the benignant "father" by recognising his claims, even as he exposed the defects of Louis XVII., and showed how impossible it would be for one brought up in a foreign land, professing a foreign religion, and used to the freedom and honour of the savage, to rule wisely and well a people who had been steeped in licentiousness and valetudinarianism for centuries.

A few years after the Prince de Joinville's visit to Green Bay Mr. Williams received a letter from Mr. Kemball, of Barton Rouge. This letter contained the dying statement of a French gentleman, named Bellanger, who had died at New Orleans, and stated that "he was the person who aided the escape of the Dauphin, or the son of Louis XVI., King of France, from the Temple in 1795; his transportation to North America, and his adoption by the Indians, that he might live and be hidden beyond the reach of his enemies; and that the person alluded to as the Dauphin was no other than the Eleazar Williams, the missionary to the Oneida Indians."

Taken in connection with the fact that Bellanger, the painter, was known to have been with the Dauphin during what were supposed to be his last days, and with the affidavit of Mrs. Margaret Brown, of New Orleans, this statement throws a very strong light upon the validity of Mr. Williams' claims, especially when it is remembered that neither Mr. Bellanger nor Mrs. Brown knew of the Prince de Joinville's visit to Green Bay, and that they each made voluntary statements, and neither was acquainted with the other.

Mrs. Brown, who was well known in New
Orleans, said that she was born in 1779. She
first married a French Republican, Benjamin
Olivier, in Edinburgh, and went with him to
France. In 1804 she was married a second
time, to Joseph Deboit, who was secretary to
the Count D'Artois, then living at Holyrood
House, Edinburgh. Shortly after their marriage
Deboit accompanied the Count to London, and
she joined him there. The Duc de Provence
and the Duchesse D'Angoulême were living in
South Audley Street in 1806-7, and Madame
Deboit saw them constantly, her position as the
wife of the Count D'Artois' secretary throwing
her into intimate relations with the Duchesse
D'Angoulême. Madame Deboit's curiosity having
been aroused by something her husband had
said, she asked the Duchesse her opinion regarding the Dauphin's fate. She replied that

"she knew he was alive and safe in America." At this time also Madame Deboit heard from one of the royal family that "it was a man named Bellanger who carried the Dauphin to America."

M. Deboit died in 1810, and in 1811 Madame Deboit went to France about some property, and at Morley she married George Brown, an American. In 1813 General Moreau gave several despatches to Mrs. Brown for the Bourbons in England, which she took to them sewed between the lining and the leather of her trunk.

Mr. Brown died in 1815, and in 1817 Mrs. Brown was living in the same house with Mrs. Chamberlau, the wife of the Count de Coigry's secretary, who had previously lived with the Duc de Provence, at Edinburgh, where Mrs. Brown had known him. Mrs. Chamberlau told her that she had heard at the Tuileries that the Dauphin was alive, and that a person by the name of Bellanger had carried him to Philadelphia, that he was known by the name of Williams, that he was a missionary to the Indians, and that the royal family considered him incompetent to reign. Mrs. Brown frequently told this story to a Mrs. Read, of New Orleans, and the Rev. Charles Whitall, and in proof of her veracity, showed a secret badge ornamented with *fleur-de-lis*, which she had had given her to pass the lines, and which she always found effectual. In connection with Mrs. Brown's story, there at once occurs to one that the last person known to have seen the Dauphin, save Gomin and Lasnè, was Bellanger, the artist to the Duc de Provence.

As to tokens of personal identity, Mr. Williams possessed many of the traits and peculiarities of the Bourbons. There are extant three pictures which bear ample testimony to this: one is a sketch of the Dauphin, taken while in prison in the Temple; the second a picture of Eleazar Williams as a young man between eighteen and twenty-one; the third a portrait of Mr. Williams, by Chevalier Fagnani, when he was over sixty years of age. The sketch of the little Dauphin is pitifully sad, showing plainly the results of imprisonment and cruelty; but the features are all the more startling in their resemblance to the young Eleazar, owing to the thin cheeks and broad brow which are identical in each.

In the portrait by Fagnani we find "the port and presence of a gentleman of high rank, a nameless something belonging only to those born to command; a countenance bronzed by exposure, a high, ample, intellectual, but receding forehead; a slightly aquiline, small nose; a long

UNIV. OF
CALIFORNIA

Austrian lip, the expression one of exceeding sweetness; full fleshy cheeks; dark bright eyes of hazel hue; dark hair sprinkled with grey; eyebrows full and of the same colour,"—a description that will at once recall the countenance of Louis XVI., and more particularly Louis XVIII.

There is one point of family resemblance that is never missing in the Bourbons, and which is characterised as the Bourbon ear; it is to be found in the portraits of Louis XVI. and XVIII., Charles X., the Duchesse D'Angoulême, and the Duc de Bordeau, just as it is found in that of Mr. Williams. The ear, large and full at the top, becomes almost a point at the lobe, and joins the cheek in one round sweep.

M. Fagnani, who had lived most of his life among the Sicilian and Spanish Bourbons, and had painted numerous portraits of them, writes thus:—" In painting the portrait of Mr. Williams,

I noticed many of the peculiarities which are developed in most of the princes of the House of Bourbon whose portraits I have taken. . . . I was most particularly impressed with his resemblance to the portraits of Louis XVI. and XVIII., and the general Bourbonic outline of his face and head. As I conversed with him I noticed several physiognomical details which rendered the resemblance to the family more striking. The upper part of the face is decidedly of a Bourbonic cast, while the mouth and lower part resemble the House of Hapsburg. I also observed, to my surprise, that many of his gestures were similar to those peculiar to the Bourbons."

M. Müller, who was the artist employed to take the portrait of Louis XVIII. after death, said on first seeing Mr. Williams, "He has the eyes of the Dauphin;" and these eyes were not the traditional blue, but the bright hazel as seen in the portrait owned by Mr. Bryan, of New York, and which had once belonged to M. Rousteau, a devoted loyalist; while people knowing the Count de Balbi, an illegitimate son of Louis XVIII., were struck with Mr. Williams' likeness to him.

Nor were these the only marks of identity. Mr. Williams bore the traces at wrists, knees, and ankles of tumours from which he had suffered as a boy, and on his arm was a curious crescent-shape inoculation mark, the same as that recorded in the "Memoirs of the Duchesse D'Angoulême" left on the Dauphin's arm after his inoculation.

These are but a few of the many strange characteristics uniting Mr. Williams with the Bourbon race. Instance after instance, might be quoted of those, strangers as well as friends, who were struck by his marked resemblance to

Louis XVI. and XVIII. A gentleman* told the writer that when he first saw Mr. Williams it gave him a physical shock, so identical was his face with that of the Bourbons; it might almost have been the countenance of the murdered Louis XVI.

It will doubtless occur to those who read this paper, that the Duchesse D'Angoulême, if she knew of her brother's escape and life among the Indians, played but a coward's part, in after years, in ignoring his existence and making no effort to procure his return; her position must, however, be borne in mind during the reign of her uncle. She was attached to him by fear and affection; to her he was always kind and considerate; and her husband was the presumable heir to the throne should Louis XVIII. die. She

---

* The present rector of Trinity Church, New York, Dr. Morgan Dix, S.T.D.

had also been taught to believe the Dauphin dead, and when the fact of his being alive was revealed to her she could only remember him as the poor idiotic child of the Temple, and wait patiently until time and opportunity made his return possible; for it is very certain that she knew nothing of her uncle's political schemes and intrigues, but was rather "the victim of his ambition." We do know that she several times declared she knew her brother to be alive, and in America ; and her persistent denials of the authenticity of Naundorf or Richmont's claims render this assertion of hers the more remarkable. How much or how little she really did know of all the terrible scenes in the Temple—the abduction of her brother, and her uncle's share in the transaction—will doubtless be made known to the world some time within the next half century, as, according to her solemn instructions, her biography, written by her own hand, is to be made public in the year 1953. Madame de Chateaubriand tells us that the Duchesse "never smiled, but went through life and to the tomb bowed down by some deep-seated and mysterious sorrow;" and who can doubt that those long nights spent in pacing her apartment were caused by the upbraiding of her heart and the impotency of her position?

We have but to glance over the Bourbon history since the French Revolution to see retribution following them step by step. No sooner did they reach the apogee of their ambition than they were thrown back into a deeper gulf than that from which they had emerged. Exile, assassination, agitation, marked their career, and "in their proudest days they were but crowned brigands, while distrust, suspicion, and fear pursued them to the last."

Mr. Williams' friends had every hope of establishing the validity of his claims to the throne of France ; his partisans held prominent positions in America, and there was no lack of the sinews of war—in this case, money—to carry on the investigations. They had so clearly demonstrated Mr. Williams' position in America, they felt confident, could strong enough pressure be brought to bear, the Continental political powers would take up the subject and enforce a settlement of it. To procure this result, Mr. Fleming, and one or two other gentlemen, obtained the consent of Lord Elgin—who was the British Commissioner to the great "World's Fair," then being held at New York—to be present at a banquet given by Mr., afterwards Sir Edward, Archibald, the English Consul-General, at which Mr. Williams was also to appear to meet Lord Elgin, when the whole matter of his claims would be laid before his lordship, and his powerful aid be asked in Mr. Williams' behalf.

And, indeed, there was something peculiarly interesting and appropriate in such an arrangement, for already Mr. Williams—as the Dauphin—was under pathetic obligations to Lord Elgin. At the time of the little Capet's imprisonment, Lord Elgin's father was Ambassador to France, and his little son was about the age of Louis XVII. Lady Elgin, whose mother's heart was deeply touched by the forlorn position of the poor little royal prisoner, was in the habit of sending, for his use, various articles of her son's clothing, and never ceased her solicitude and care until forced to do so by untoward circumstances. The very little "grey coat" spoken of by Lamartine may have belonged to the famous Lord Elgin, to whom the world owes such a debt of gratitude.

It is not difficult then to imagine what would have been the character of such a meeting between the two men, or how eagerly Mr. Williams' friends must have looked forward to Lord Elgin's sympathy and strength in their behalf. The little Capet had grown to man's estate, and become the victim of a cruel fate, since he wore the boyish habiliments of his quondam friend; while Lord Elgin had risen to the height of his fame, and was a power in that world which should have recognised the other's claims.

Unfortunately the meeting never took place. While still on board ship Lord Elgin was attacked with violent gout, and was not only unable to attend the dinner, but could not land when the ship reached New York. The disappointment was a bitter one to the hopes of Mr. Williams' party, and soon after Mr. Fleming, for personal reasons, being unable to go on with the investigations,— to which he had devoted not only his time, but his money, with unstinted generosity,—they were discontinued.

Mr. Williams lived and died in obscurity. His fortune fell from him, his adopted country but scantily rewarded his services in its behalf, his Indian flock time and again repudiated his care, he was persecuted by those whom he had aided, and every sorrow that human nature is prone to devolved upon him, but did not crush him. His faith was too firmly rooted, his belief in an Almighty Power too strong, to be overcome by worldly vicissitudes; and equally firm was his belief in his royal birth and his just claims to the throne of France. No amount of falsehood, calumny, unfaithfulness, or derision could shake this belief; and in this very firmness he displayed a characteristic of his race. He felt himself unfitted to reign over France; his entire life, since his adoption—training, religion, and associations—was antagonistic to a life of power. He never desired greatness, but he did desire his parentage and lineage to be proved to the world; and though this tardy justice was denied him, save by his partizans, he still kept to the "even tenor of his way." Nothing could shake his belief in himself, and he bore himself to the last day of his life with the calm dignity of royalty, and the gentleness of a man of God.

His journal, which for many years was the reflex of his inner life, is one strong link in the strange chain of his eventful existence; the very peculiarities of its style, the foreign idioms used unconsciously, add to its reality, and point to far different surroundings in his early life before he lost his mind, or in later years became a teacher of the red man. Unlike Naundorf, he frankly admitted that all recollection of his childhood was gone from him; he remembered nothing until after his accident at Lake George; but at that time, before he came to manhood or into the notice of others, he told of the strange and often terrible visions that haunted him.

How different is this to the glib and perfect memory of Naundorf, who told his tale to suit his audience, and who three times changed it before it reached the ears of the Duchesse D'Angoulême.

Which would be the most natural outcome of the cruelty bestowed upon the Dauphin in the Temple—a cruelty that reduced him to imbecility—the frank acknowledgment of the loss of all recollection of childhood admitted by Mr. Williams, or the precocious knowledge displayed by Naundorf? The answer is obvious.

It may be asked, Of what good is this recapitulation of events and lives long since ended, against whose crimes and inconsistencies *Finis* has been written these many years? Since the actors are dead and the scenes shifted, why bring back the unfinished drama and ask an ending to it from these days of unbelief and scepticism?

Granted the answer remains unsatisfactory, for who can prove that Louis XVII. of France and Mr. Eleazar Williams are one and the same; yet who can disprove it? Who has solved the mystery of the Man in the Iron Mask? May not we all have our own surmises and theories?

There is, however, this fact to be borne in mind. Mr. Williams, unlike Naundorf or Richemont, never sought himself to bring forward his claim; but those who knew him were so assured of its validity, they felt no sacrifice, on their parts, would be too great to ensure its recognition. Again, his friends and partizans were not of that class who might hope for some personal aggrandisement, were they successful; on the contrary, they were found among the most intellectual, the most scholarly, the most prominent men of the day; each profession was represented by one of its most leading members, and not one of them ever doubted Mr. Williams' absolute right to the throne of France; it was only untoward circumstances that caused their investigations to be stopped.

Mr. Williams was innocent of any desire for publicity, and was both astonished and distressed when his friends' belief in his identity with the Dauphin forced him before the public; but once his own mind was made up as to the validity of his claim, he could not but wish to have it established in the eyes of the public. He was the most devoted of missionaries, and loved his Indian flock with all his heart; his greatest desire was their advancement, and he only cared for riches that he might expend them upon his dusky children.

It will, then, readily be seen how very different was his position and conduct to that of Naundorf, and how brightly, throughout all circumstances, shines his modesty and humility, in contrast to the other's cupidity and self-assertion.

In putting forth this small portion of the facts and coincidences relative to the Dauphin and Mr. Williams, and which are at least "passing strange," the writer leaves to every one their own opinion upon them; but when they look upon the Indians of the Wild West, and see their fine physique, and observe their stoical, dignified carriage and calm indifferent faces, they may well recall the story of the lost Prince, and grant that if Louis XVII. did live and die a missionary to the Oneida and St. Regis tribes, his fate may perhaps have been a happier one than had he recovered his father's throne, since at least he was spared the uneasiness of him who wears a crown, the curse of a "barren sceptre," and a life of unrealities.

THE END.

Printed by Hazell, Watson, & Viney, Ld., London and Aylesbury.

www.ingramcontent.com/pod-product-compliance
Lightning Source LLC
Chambersburg PA
CBHW022137160426
43197CB00009B/1320